Driving Change

Driving Change

INNOVATING SUSTAINABILITY IN THE AUTOMOTIVE INDUSTRY

Anurag Anurag

Contents

1

∽

Introduction to Sustainability in the Automotive Industry

In the bustling world of automotive innovation, where the roar of engines and the sleek designs of new models capture the imagination, there lies a pressing need—a drive towards sustainability. As climate change accelerates and resources dwindle, the automotive industry stands at a pivotal crossroads: continue on the path of traditional manufacturing with its environmental toll or pivot towards a more sustainable future. This book aims to explore how the industry can not only navigate this transition but also lead the way in environmental stewardship.

The importance of sustainability in the automotive industry cannot be overstated. Vehicles are among the major contributors to global carbon emissions, accounting for a significant portion of air pollution in urban environments. Moreover, the manufacturing processes involved in producing cars consume vast amounts of materials and energy, often sourced from non-renewable resources. Addressing these impacts is not just an environmental imperative but an economic and social one as well, influencing everything from global policy to individual consumer choices.

This chapter sets the stage for a comprehensive discussion on sustainable practices within the automotive industry. It will delve into the historical development of the industry, its current challenges and opportunities for sustainability, and highlight the innovations that are making a difference. From alternative fuels and advancements in electric vehicles to improvements in manufacturing processes and materials, the book will cover a range of topics that are central to the transformation of the automotive landscape.

By understanding the role of sustainability in today's automotive industry, readers will be better equipped to appreciate the complex interplay of engineering, design, and environmental science that is shaping the future of transportation. This book is not just a recount of what has been done; it is a guide to what can be done and a call to action for all stakeholders involved, from manufacturers to consumers, to drive change towards a more sustainable and environmentally responsible automotive future.

As we delve deeper into the possibilities of a more sustainable automotive future, it becomes essential to consider not only the theoretical aspects but also practical examples that illustrate the successful integration of sustainability in the automotive industry. One notable instance is the progression of electric vehicles (EVs) led by companies like Tesla, which have not only advanced the technology but also reshaped consumer perceptions and industry standards regarding what environmentally friendly vehicles can achieve.

Tesla's approach to integrating high-capacity batteries and efficient motors has set benchmarks in the EV industry, showing that electric cars can offer performance and convenience without the environmental footprint of traditional combustion engines. Moreover, Tesla's investment in a comprehensive charging infrastructure has helped overcome one of the biggest hurdles facing electric vehicle adoption, demonstrating a holistic approach to promoting sustainable automotive technology.

Another significant example involves the use of recycled materials in car manufacturing. Companies like BMW and Toyota are pioneering the use of sustainable materials in their vehicles. BMW's i3, for instance, features door panels made from recycled plastics and renewable resources such as kenaf, a plant similar to jute, which reduces the weight and, consequently, the energy consumption of the vehicle. Toyota has also been a leader in using bio-based materials, incorporating substances like sugarcane-derived bio-PE (polyethylene) in their vehicles, which significantly reduces the carbon footprint associated with production.

Moreover, advancements in manufacturing efficiency also play a crucial role. Ford's implementation of 3D printing for non-critical parts not only reduces the waste generated during manufacturing but also allows for lighter, more energy-efficient vehicles. These examples highlight not just the advancements in technology but also the increasing importance of sustainable practices in reducing environmental impact while still meeting consumer demands and regulatory requirements.

By exploring these cases, this chapter provides a glimpse into the practical application of sustainable innovations in the automotive industry. These examples are not just isolated incidents but are part of a broader movement towards environmental stewardship that is becoming increasingly central to the automotive sector's business models and strategies. This shift is not merely about compliance or marketing but about paving the way for a sustainable future that aligns with global efforts to mitigate environmental degradation and promote a healthier planet.

2

∽

History of Automotive Industry and Environmental Impact

The history of the automotive industry is a tale of innovation, economic transformation, and significant environmental impact. From the production of the first gasoline-powered automobiles to the rise of global automotive giants, the industry has been a major driver of technological and economic progress. However, this progress has come at a substantial environmental cost, marked by increased greenhouse gas emissions, extensive resource consumption, and significant pollution.

The 20th century saw a boom in automotive production, primarily fueled by the availability of cheap oil and the mass-production techniques pioneered by Henry Ford. Cars became symbols of personal freedom and economic status, but this growth led to rising concerns over air pollution, oil dependency, and carbon emissions. Cities around the world began to experience smog and deteriorating air quality, directly linked to increasing vehicle numbers.

In response to these environmental challenges, the industry started to see shifts in the late 20th and early 21st centuries. One pivotal moment was the oil crisis of the 1970s, which spurred initial interest in fuel efficiency and alternative energy sources. This crisis highlighted the vulnerabilities of heavy reliance on fossil fuels and sparked the development of more fuel-efficient vehicles, including early prototypes of electric and hybrid cars.

Examples of significant shifts toward sustainability include the Toyota Prius and the Chevrolet Volt. The Toyota Prius, introduced in 1997, became a symbol of eco-friendly technology with its hybrid engine, significantly reducing fuel consumption and emissions compared to conventional vehicles. The Chevrolet Volt further advanced this trend by combining an electric motor with a gasoline engine, allowing for longer electric-only driving distances and less frequent fuel use.

Moreover, regulatory changes have played a crucial role in pushing the industry towards sustainability. The introduction of emission standards in major markets like the United States and the European Union forced automakers to develop cleaner, more efficient technologies. These regulations have led to innovations in engine design, lightweight materials, and even the incorporation of recycled materials into new vehicles, demonstrating a comprehensive approach to reducing environmental impacts.

The history of the automotive industry is a vivid illustration of innovation and economic transformation, paralleled by significant environmental repercussions. As the 20th century unfolded, the widespread adoption of the automobile revolutionized personal mobility and spurred economic growth but also brought about substantial environmental challenges, such as increased greenhouse gas emissions, resource depletion, and significant air and noise pollution.

The industrial surge led by figures like Henry Ford, who pioneered mass production techniques, made automobiles affordable and ubiquitous. This accessibility changed the societal landscape but also escalated oil consumption and emissions. By the mid-20th century, cities around the world were experiencing the adverse effects of automotive pollution, with smog and deteriorating air quality becoming common concerns.

The environmental consciousness of the 1960s and 1970s marked a pivotal shift in public and governmental attitudes towards automotive emissions. The oil crises of the 1970s acted as a critical wake-up call, highlighting the unsustainable nature of fossil fuel dependence. This period spurred initial investments and interest in alternative energy sources and marked the beginning of regulatory frameworks aimed at reducing automotive emissions.

Examples of industry responses to these pressures include the development of the catalytic converter, an innovation introduced in the mid-1970s to reduce harmful emissions from gasoline engines. This device was a direct result of new regulations like the Clean Air Act in the United States, which mandated reductions in automobile emissions.

Technological innovations such as the introduction of the Toyota Prius in 1997 showcased the industry's capability to integrate sustainability into its products. The Prius, as the world's first mass-produced hybrid vehicle, represented a major step forward in reducing fuel consumption and emissions and became a symbol of eco-friendly automotive technology. Similarly, the Chevrolet Volt, introduced in 2010, pushed the boundaries further by combining an electric motor with a gasoline engine, which allowed for extended electric-only propulsion and reduced gasoline consumption.

In addition to technological advancements, the automotive industry's journey toward sustainability has been significantly influenced by changing regulatory landscapes. Stricter emission standards and fuel efficiency requirements in major markets such as the European Union, the United States, and Japan have driven automakers to innovate aggressively in clean technologies. These regulations have not only prompted improvements in traditional internal combustion engines but have also accelerated the development and adoption of alternative propulsion systems like electric and hydrogen fuel cell vehicles.

These historical insights set the stage for an in-depth exploration of current sustainability challenges and innovations in the automotive industry. By understanding this complex background, readers gain a comprehensive view of how deeply intertwined economic, technological, and environmental factors are in shaping the future direction of automotive development and sustainability efforts. This narrative underscores the urgency and importance of the industry's shift towards more sustainable practices, which will be further explored in subsequent chapters.

The automotive industry's response to environmental challenges has not only been reactive but also proactive, with significant investments in research and development leading to groundbreaking innovations. For instance, the development of fuel cell technology, which combines hydrogen and oxygen to produce electricity without combustion, offers a glimpse into potential future mainstream solutions that could drastically reduce vehicular emissions. Companies like Honda with their Clarity Fuel Cell vehicle have pioneered this technology, demonstrating its viability in real-world conditions.

Moreover, advancements in digital technology have enabled better efficiency and lower emissions. Vehicle telematics systems that monitor engine performance, vehicle speed, and fuel consumption in real-time provide valuable data that can be used to optimize vehicle operations and reduce emissions. Such systems are becoming increasingly common in new vehicles, driven by both consumer demand for better fuel efficiency and tighter emissions regulations.

The push for more sustainable automotive practices has also led to significant changes in vehicle design and construction. Automakers are increasingly adopting lightweight materials such as aluminum and carbon fiber to reduce the overall weight of vehicles, thereby enhancing fuel efficiency and reducing emissions. For example, Ford's use of aluminum in the body of its F-150 pickup truck marks one of the most significant shifts towards lightweight construction in mainstream vehicles.

At the same time, regulatory bodies worldwide are tightening emissions standards, compelling automakers to accelerate the development of cleaner technologies. The European Union's stringent Euro 6 standards, the United States' Corporate Average Fuel Economy (CAFE) standards, and China's ambitious fuel consumption standards for passenger cars all exemplify the global trend towards stricter environmental regulation.

Consumer awareness and demand for sustainable and environmentally friendly vehicles have grown exponentially. This shift is partly due to more accessible information on the environmental impact of personal vehicle use and a stronger societal focus on combating climate change. As a result, consumers are increasingly favoring vehicles with lower emissions, better fuel efficiency, and minimal environmental impact, driving automakers to prioritize sustainability in their new models.

The convergence of these factors—technological innovation, regulatory pressures, and evolving consumer preferences—is crafting a new paradigm in the automotive industry. This holistic approach to sustainability is poised to transform not just how vehicles are made and used but also how they are perceived in the broader context of global environmental health. As this chapter elaborates on these themes, it paints a comprehensive picture of an industry at a pivotal moment, ready to embrace a future where sustainability is no longer an option but a necessity.

As this chapter concludes, it is clear that the automotive industry stands at a significant crossroads. The convergence of technological innovation, stringent regulatory pressures, and shifting consumer preferences is driving an unprecedented transformation towards sustainability. The industry's journey from the first gasoline-powered automobiles to today's electric and hydrogen fuel cell vehicles reflects a profound shift in the global automotive landscape. This evolution is not just about adhering to environmental standards but about pioneering a future where mobility is both sustainable and beneficial for society at large.

The narrative we have traced in this chapter—from the industrial surge of the 20th century to the current embrace of cutting-edge technologies—illustrates a dynamic industry that is responsive and responsible. Automakers are no longer merely manufacturers of vehicles but are architects of comprehensive mobility solutions. They are crafting vehicles that are cleaner, smarter, and more integrated into the fabric of an eco-conscious world.

This chapter has also highlighted that while technology and innovation are crucial, the path to a sustainable automotive industry is paved with collaborative efforts. Governments, consumers, manufacturers, and multiple stakeholders across the globe need to continue working together to foster an environment where sustainable practices are nurtured and flourish.

In summary, the transformation of the automotive industry is both a challenge and an opportunity—an opportunity to redefine the essence of mobility and to ensure that this redefinition is aligned with the long-term health of our planet. The industry's commitment to this goal will undoubtedly continue to inspire innovations, influence global policies, and shape consumer attitudes towards a more sustainable future.

3

Current Challenges and Opportunities

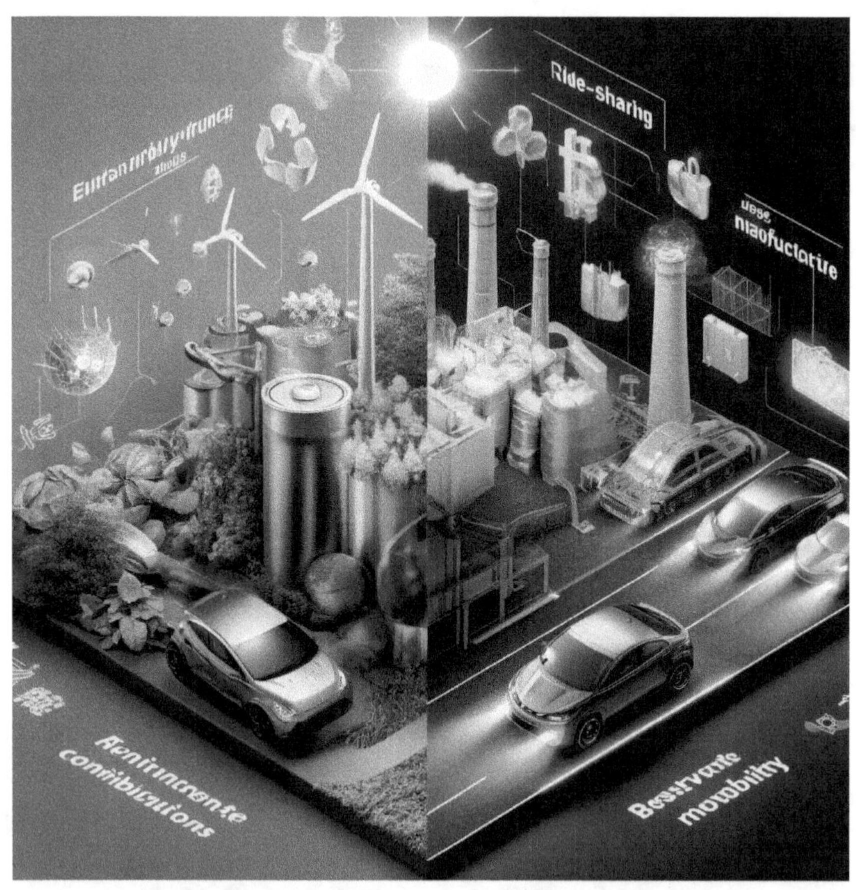

As the automotive industry navigates the 21st century, it faces a myriad of challenges coupled with a horizon rich in opportunities. The push for sustainability sits at the forefront of industry concerns, with climate change accelerating the imperative for reduced carbon emissions. This environmental urgency intersects with the practicalities of economics, consumer demands, and technological evolution, creating a complex battlefield for industry players.

The tightening grip of global emissions standards compels a re-evaluation of the combustion engine's viability, urging a transition to low-emission vehicles. In this struggle, electric vehicles (EVs) emerge as beacons of hope, their once-niche presence swelling into a significant market force. However, the shift is not without its hurdles. The EV revolution grapples with challenges such as the development of robust charging infrastructure, ensuring energy for these new fleets is drawn from renewable sources, and addressing the environmental impact of battery production and disposal.

Resource scarcity further intensifies the industry's trials, particularly concerning rare earth materials vital for EV batteries and electronic components. Automakers are prompted to innovate in recycling and material recovery, to not only mitigate environmental impacts but also to insulate themselves against volatile commodity markets.

Yet, within these challenges, opportunities abound. Advances in battery technology, including solid-state batteries, offer the potential for longer ranges, shorter charging times, and safer chemistries, which could significantly lower the barriers to EV adoption. Autonomous driving technology, while still in its infancy, presents another frontier with the potential to revolutionize vehicle efficiency and road safety.

On the manufacturing front, sustainable practices are gaining traction. From reducing water usage and waste to integrating recycled materials into new vehicles, manufacturers are finding ways to minimize their ecological footprint. In parallel, the emergence of sharing economy models and mobility-as-a-service (MaaS) provides a glimpse into a future with potentially fewer cars on the road, reducing overall environmental impact.

The automotive industry's journey is no longer just about mobility but about carving a path that is both sustainable and beneficial for the planet. The current era is marked by a transition from merely selling vehicles to offering integrated and sustainable mobility solutions. The challenges are significant, but the collective resolve and innovative spirit of the industry promise a road ahead paved with transformative potential. This chapter is not only a recount of current issues but also a canvas for painting the picture of an evolving industry that seeks to harmonize the rhythm of human progress with the delicate cadences of our environment.

The contemporary automotive landscape is rich with examples that illustrate both the challenges faced and the opportunities grasped. A prominent example is the struggle to balance the ecological footprint of battery production with the environmental benefits of electric vehicles. The production of lithium-ion batteries, the heart of electric cars, involves mining of lithium, cobalt, and nickel, raising concerns about ecological degradation and ethical sourcing. Companies like Tesla are seeking to address these challenges head-on, with CEO Elon Musk announcing initiatives to source raw materials more sustainably and to advance battery recycling techniques.

Further afield, Volvo has committed to becoming climate neutral by 2040, not only by electrifying its range but by overhauling its manufacturing processes. Its ambitious plans include reducing the lifecycle carbon footprint per car by 40% by 2025. In a similar vein, BMW has pioneered the use of renewable materials and recycling in its manufacturing, with models featuring recycled plastics and renewable resources, setting a precedent for circular economy principles in automotive design.

Another testament to the industry's adaptive capabilities is seen in the rise of ride-sharing services like Uber and Lyft. These platforms have introduced a shift in consumer behavior, emphasizing access over ownership, and inadvertently contributing to the reduction of vehicles on the road. However, they also present a new challenge: the increase in traffic congestion and emissions in urban areas. This has prompted these companies to invest in electric fleets and explore partnerships with public transit systems to create more sustainable urban transportation ecosystems.

Simultaneously, technological innovation in autonomous driving promises to redefine vehicle usage. Google's Waymo, through its autonomous driving trials, is not just aiming to revolutionize safety but also to improve vehicle efficiency and reduce idle times, leading to lower emissions.

The narrative of the automotive industry is no longer just about horsepower and aesthetics but increasingly about energy efficiency, ethical sourcing, and sustainability. Companies are exploring synthetic fuels and hydrogen power as potential complements or alternatives to electric powertrains, promising a diversified approach to sustainable mobility. This chapter narrates not just a story of challenges and responses but also of a profound transformation shaping the essence of mobility for a sustainable future.

As the automotive industry embraces new technologies and shifts towards sustainability, the workforce must adapt to new roles and skills. The rise of electric vehicles requires expertise in battery technology and electrical systems, differing significantly from traditional automotive skills focused on internal combustion engines. This transition represents a challenge for current employees but also an opportunity for job creation in new segments of the industry, such as battery production and renewable energy integration.

Moreover, the industry's shift impacts the broader socio-economic landscape, influencing everything from urban planning to global supply chains. As cities adopt more sustainable transportation solutions, there is an increased need for urban planners and policymakers who understand the dynamics of electric and autonomous vehicles within public infrastructure. The move towards localized production and supply chains to reduce environmental impact further stimulates local economies but requires careful management to ensure that the benefits are widely distributed.

Consumer behavior and societal trends also play a significant role in shaping the industry's direction. The growing consumer preference for sustainability is driving companies to prioritize green practices not only in vehicle production but throughout their corporate operations. This shift is influenced by a more informed and environmentally conscious consumer base, pushing automakers to increase transparency and accountability in their environmental commitments.

The industry's response to these socio-economic challenges is multifaceted. Companies are investing in training and development programs to ensure their workforce can meet the demands of new technologies. Partnerships between automakers, educational institutions, and governments are fostering the growth of specialized training programs that focus on the skills needed in a more electric and digital automotive market.

Additionally, as the industry moves towards more integrated and intelligent mobility solutions, there is a growing emphasis on data security and privacy. The increased connectivity of vehicles raises concerns about data breaches and the potential misuse of personal information. This aspect of automotive technology development requires robust cybersecurity measures and clear regulations to protect consumers, highlighting the need for ongoing collaboration between industry players, tech companies, and regulatory bodies.

The automotive industry's journey towards sustainability is complex and interwoven with technological, economic, and social threads. Each advancement in technology not only brings new opportunities but also challenges that must be managed to ensure that the shift towards sustainable mobility benefits all sectors of society. The future of the automotive industry is not just about greener vehicles but about creating a more sustainable world through innovative mobility solutions and responsible corporate practices.

Environmental sustainability in the automotive industry extends into the realm of end-of-life vehicle management. The industry is increasingly focusing on how vehicles can be designed for easier disassembly and recycling, reducing landfill waste and promoting a circular economy. Innovations in this area include modular designs that allow for easier replacement and recycling of parts. Companies like Toyota are pioneering these efforts with their eco-friendly design and manufacturing processes that ensure that up to 95% of their vehicles are recyclable.

The impact of new mobility solutions on traditional car ownership models is profound. Car-sharing and subscription services are reshaping consumer attitudes towards ownership, promoting a usage-based model rather than personal ownership. This not only reduces the number of vehicles needed but also decreases the urban space required for parking, contributing to lower urban congestion and pollution. Companies like Zipcar and even traditional automakers with subscription services are at the forefront of this shift, offering flexible transportation solutions that align with a more sustainable urban lifestyle.

Additionally, the integration of electric vehicles into the energy grid as mobile storage units presents an innovative way to manage renewable energy resources more effectively. Known as Vehicle-to-Grid (V2G) technology, this approach allows energy stored in electric vehicle batteries to be fed back into the grid during peak demand times. This not only helps stabilize the grid but also ensures that renewable energy generation can be optimized and utilized more efficiently.

Global cooperation is crucial in scaling sustainable practices across the industry. International agreements and partnerships can help standardize regulations and foster the exchange of technology and best practices. For example, the Paris Agreement has been a pivotal global initiative influencing national policies and industry practices towards reducing carbon emissions. The automotive industry's commitment to this and similar agreements showcases its role in global efforts to combat climate change.

In wrapping up the discussion on the future of the automotive industry, it is essential to recognize the role of innovation in driving sustainability. Breakthroughs in material science, energy storage, and artificial intelligence are continually shaping the capabilities and impact of vehicles. The industry's forward-looking approach is not only about adapting to the changes but also about being a proactive player in the global shift towards sustainability.

By continuing to innovate and adapt, the automotive industry is poised to overcome its environmental challenges and lead the way in sustainable practices. The concerted effort of manufacturers, consumers, policymakers, and researchers is creating a robust framework for a future where mobility is efficient, environmentally friendly, and accessible to all. This collective journey towards sustainability in the automotive industry is a testament to the power of human ingenuity and commitment to planetary stewardship.

4

Sustainable Design and Materials

In the quest for sustainability, the automotive industry is increasingly focusing on sustainable design and the use of eco-friendly materials. This chapter explores the intricate dance of form and function, where the drive for efficiency and the need to reduce environmental impact shape the very materials and designs that make up modern vehicles.

Designers and engineers are now tasked with the complex challenge of creating cars that are not only aesthetically pleasing and performant but also environmentally conscious. This has led to innovative approaches to both the external aerodynamics and internal features of vehicles. By optimizing the shape and form of cars, automakers can significantly reduce drag, which in turn enhances fuel efficiency and reduces emissions. Companies like Tesla have mastered this art, producing vehicles with some of the lowest drag coefficients in the industry.

When it comes to materials, the change is even more profound. The traditional steel and plastics are being increasingly replaced or complemented by alternative materials. BMW's 'i' series, for example, utilizes carbon fiber-reinforced plastic to drastically reduce weight without compromising safety. This not only enhances efficiency but also lowers the carbon footprint of the production process.

Interior elements are also witnessing a green overhaul. Ford, among others, has pioneered the use of soy foam in seats and other interior components. Similarly, recycled materials are becoming a staple in the interior design of many cars. Nissan's Leaf uses fabrics made entirely from recycled water bottles, while the luxury car manufacturer Jaguar Land Rover is using Econyl, a fabric made from ocean waste, to upholster interiors.

The path forward is paved with innovations such as bioplastics, which are plastics made from plant biomass rather than petroleum, and the use of natural fiber composites. Research into materials like hemp, flax, and kenaf is yielding promising results, showing that these materials can be used to make strong, lightweight components for vehicle interiors and even body panels.

The push for sustainability is also leading to an emphasis on the life-cycle of vehicles. Manufacturers are beginning to design cars with the end of their life in mind, focusing on how each part can be recycled or repurposed. The aim is to create a circular economy within the automotive industry, where waste is minimized and materials are continuously reused.

In this chapter, we see the automotive industry at a crossroads, where every decision made in the design and material selection process can have a significant impact on the environment. The shift to sustainable design and materials is not a mere trend but a fundamental change that will define the future of automotive manufacturing. The direction is clear: to continue to innovate, to reduce our reliance on non-renewable resources, and to create vehicles that are kinder to the planet they traverse.

Sustainable design and materials are at the heart of a transformative shift in the automotive industry. In recent years, we have witnessed an increase in the use of aluminum, which, while not new to the industry, is being utilized more extensively to reduce weight and, consequently, emissions. The Audi A8, for example, boasts a body made almost entirely of aluminum, setting a benchmark for lightweight construction.

Beyond lightweight metals, the industry is also exploring bio-based materials. Toyota's use of bioplastics, derived from sugarcane and corn, in its Prius model, is a testament to this trend. These materials not only reduce the vehicle's environmental impact but also serve as a stepping stone towards a more sustainable supply chain.

The concept of 'design for disassembly' is gaining momentum, with companies designing vehicles that can be easily taken apart at the end of their lifecycle. This approach facilitates recycling and reusing parts, further enhancing the sustainability of the manufacturing process. For instance, Volvo's electric vehicle battery design allows for the battery to be disassembled and the materials within it to be reused, reducing waste and the demand for new raw materials.

In the realm of luxury cars, Tesla's vegan leather interiors provide an alternative to traditional leather, offering a cruelty-free and more sustainable option that does not compromise on quality or comfort. This move is not just about meeting the demands of eco-conscious consumers but also about redefining luxury in the context of sustainability.

The push for sustainability extends to the supply chain as well. Automakers are scrutinizing their suppliers to ensure that the materials sourced are produced responsibly. This includes ensuring fair labor practices and minimal environmental impact from the extraction and processing of materials.

As we forge ahead, the role of technological innovation in sustainable materials continues to expand. Advances in material science promise the development of new composites that are both environmentally friendly and superior in performance to their traditional counterparts. The integration of digital design tools enables more precise and efficient use of materials, reducing waste during the production phase.

The automotive industry's trajectory toward sustainable design and materials is not merely a reaction to external pressures but a proactive stride towards a more responsible form of mobility. It's a journey that necessitates a holistic view, considering the environmental impact of every aspect of a vehicle's design and life cycle. This chapter not only narrates the current state of sustainable design and materials but also serves as a manifesto for the road ahead, underlining the industry's commitment to innovation and ecological responsibility.

The industry's movement towards sustainable design is further catalyzed by a global consumer base that is increasingly environmentally aware and demands green alternatives. This consumer pressure drives manufacturers to prioritize sustainability not just as an afterthought but as a primary focus in the vehicle development process.

One of the most innovative responses to this demand is the development of 'closed-loop' recycling systems. For example, Jaguar Land Rover has implemented a process whereby aluminum from old vehicles is recycled back into the production of new cars, significantly reducing waste and the energy required to produce new aluminum.

Paints and coatings are another area where sustainability is taking center stage. Traditional automotive paints contain volatile organic compounds (VOCs) that contribute to air pollution. To address this, manufacturers are developing water-based paints that significantly reduce or eliminate the use of harmful chemicals. BMW's 'i' series uses a water-based paint process, which drastically cuts down VOC emissions during the painting phase.

Tire manufacturers are also rethinking their products. Michelin has set an ambitious goal to make tires 100% sustainable by 2050, combining natural rubber with recycled materials, and even investigating the use of wood chips as a raw material. Such initiatives, if successful, could revolutionize the tire industry and significantly decrease the environmental impact of a vehicle's consumables.

In the electric vehicle sector, battery technology remains a focal point. Manufacturers are researching ways to extend battery life, reduce charging times, and use less impactful materials. The concept of 'battery as a service' is also emerging, where the battery is leased separately from the vehicle, making EVs more affordable and facilitating easier battery recycling or upgrading.

Looking forward, the industry acknowledges that the road to

sustainability is continuous and demands persistent innovation. Bio-degradable materials, solar body panels, and energy-harvesting suspension systems are no longer just speculative concepts but areas of active research and development.

In writing this chapter, it becomes clear that the future of automotive design hinges on a delicate balance between innovation, practicality, and ecological ethics. With each design decision and material selection, the industry moves a step closer to a more sustainable future, one that promises to transform the fundamental nature of transportation and its environmental impact. The industry's commitment to this transformation will undoubtedly shape the landscape of mobility for generations to come.

5

Green Manufacturing Processes

The transition to green manufacturing processes is pivotal for the automotive industry's sustainable evolution. In this chapter, we'll explore how manufacturers are rethinking production lines, adopting eco-friendly practices, and implementing technologies to reduce environmental footprints.

Green manufacturing in the automotive industry encompasses a range of practices, from reducing energy consumption and minimizing waste to using renewable energy and sustainable materials. A key component is the lifecycle assessment, evaluating the environmental impact of a vehicle from production to disposal, leading to a more eco-conscious manufacturing approach.

One of the front runners in this initiative is BMW, with its 'i' factories in Leipzig, Germany, which are designed to optimize energy efficiency and resource conservation. The factory boasts an on-site wind farm that generates the electricity needed for the production of BMW's electric 'i' series vehicles. This not only reduces the carbon footprint of the manufacturing process but also signals a shift towards self-sufficiency in energy use.

Tesla, an archetype of innovation in green manufacturing, has set high standards with its Gigafactory in Nevada. Aimed at battery production for its electric vehicles, the Gigafactory is designed to be powered entirely by renewable energy sources, with a goal to achieve net-zero energy. Tesla's approach to manufacturing extends beyond the factory walls, with initiatives to source materials ethically and to create a closed-loop system for battery recycling.

Another exemplary case is Ford's River Rouge Plant, which features a living roof - the largest in the industry. This green roof helps control heating and cooling costs, reduces stormwater runoff, and increases biodiversity. Inside the plant, Ford employs 3D printing for prototyping, saving on material costs and reducing waste.

Toyota's production system, renowned for its efficiency, has incorporated sustainable practices, including reducing water usage and solvent emissions. The Toyota Environmental Challenge 2050 outlines ambitious goals, including zero carbon emissions from its factories and a challenge to go beyond zero environmental impact to achieve a net positive impact.

In Europe, Volkswagen's 'Think Blue. Factory.' initiative demonstrates a commitment to reducing the environmental impact of its manufacturing by 25% by 2025, focusing on energy and water consumption, waste production, and CO2 emissions. Volkswagen plants have seen significant investments in energy-efficient technologies and the use of renewable energy sources.

Swedish carmaker Volvo has also taken significant strides, aiming to be climate neutral by 2040. A significant part of this goal involves transforming its manufacturing process, focusing on energy efficiency and zero-emission production plants.

Green manufacturing is not just a buzzword; it's a comprehensive approach to production that respects and preserves the environment while maintaining efficiency and profitability. It's an approach that necessitates a paradigm shift in the very philosophy of manufacturing, weaving sustainability into the core of all operations.

At the crux of green manufacturing is energy use. Traditional automotive plants are power-hungry entities, but with the advent of smart grid technologies and the integration of renewable energy sources, factories are becoming greener. For instance, General Motors' assembly plant in Joinville, Brazil, is powered by energy generated from biomass sourced from local wood waste, a renewable resource that also reduces landfill waste.

Waste reduction is another cornerstone of green manufacturing. The concept of zero waste — the design and management of processes that completely eliminate waste or convert it to new uses — is gaining traction. Nissan's plant in Smyrna, Tennessee, is one such example, having achieved a zero-waste status by repurposing all materials for alternate uses or recycling them.

Water conservation is equally significant. The production of a single car can require up to 100,000 gallons of water, but through the use of advanced treatment systems and water recycling processes, manufacturers like Toyota are dramatically reducing their water footprint. In its plants, Toyota uses a system that recycles water for multiple uses, cutting down water consumption by millions of gallons annually.

The paint shop, traditionally one of the most polluting facets of car manufacturing, is being transformed by the use of powder coatings and waterborne paints, reducing the emission of volatile organic compounds (VOCs). BMW's 'EcoPaint' process aims to optimize the painting sequence to reduce paint waste and use fewer resources.

In the realm of materials, there's a focus on not just using sustainable materials but also on sustainable sourcing. Ford, for instance, has explored the use of soy-based foams, and recycled and renewable materials such as wheat straw-reinforced plastic, finding that these materials offer significant environmental benefits without compromising quality or durability.

The green manufacturing process also emphasizes worker wellbeing and productivity, as seen in the ergonomic design of production lines and the use of collaborative robots, or cobots, which assist workers in repetitive or dangerous tasks while also improving efficiency.

Supply chain management is an essential aspect of green manufacturing. Companies are not only optimizing their own operations but are also holding suppliers to the same environmental standards, thus magnifying the positive impact. This is evident in the Responsible Business Alliance's (RBA) Code of Conduct, which many automotive companies endorse, ensuring that their supply chains are socially responsible and environmentally sound.

Implementing these green processes often requires significant upfront investment. However, the return on investment can be substantial, not just in terms of reduced operational costs but also in brand value, as consumers increasingly favor environmentally responsible companies.

Advanced manufacturing technologies such as additive manufacturing (3D printing) have revolutionized production lines, allowing for more precise material usage and significantly less waste. For instance, BMW has employed 3D printing to produce parts that are not only lighter but also reduce the number of raw materials used during manufacturing. This reduction in material waste contributes directly to environmental sustainability and aligns with the industry's broader goals.

Moreover, the deployment of automation and robotics in manufacturing processes further enhances energy efficiency. Robots are not only more precise, but they can also operate at a constant rate without the need for breaks, reducing the energy fluctuations associated with human-operated machinery. Additionally, automated systems are often more efficient in managing resources, including electricity and raw materials, which can lead to significant reductions in a plant's environmental impact.

Energy management systems are another critical aspect of modern green manufacturing. These systems monitor and control the energy use of machinery and lighting, ensuring that energy is only used when necessary and at optimal levels. For example, Renault's plants in Europe are equipped with sophisticated energy management systems that have drastically reduced their carbon footprint and improved overall energy efficiency.

The use of renewable energy sources in automotive manufacturing plants is becoming increasingly common. Companies like Tesla have pioneered the integration of solar energy into their Gigafactories, where large solar arrays contribute to the factories' power needs, moving towards a goal of net-zero energy consumption. Similarly, other manufacturers are exploring wind, geothermal, and biomass energy solutions to power their operations sustainably.

Sustainable supply chain practices are also integral to green manufacturing. Automakers are scrutinizing their supply chains more closely, ensuring that their suppliers adhere to sustainable practices. This includes managing the sustainability of the materials supplied, the environmental practices of the suppliers, and the ethical implications of sourcing decisions. For example, Volvo's commitment to using only sustainably sourced materials by 2030 has pushed their suppliers to adopt greener practices and technologies.

Finally, the water conservation efforts within automotive manufacturing cannot be overstated. Companies like Toyota have implemented sophisticated water recycling systems that not only reduce water use but also treat wastewater to a level that is often cleaner than when it was originally sourced. These efforts are crucial in regions where water scarcity is a significant issue, and they demonstrate the automotive industry's commitment to responsible environmental stewardship.

6

Alternative Fuels and Technologies

As the automotive industry accelerates towards a sustainable future, the exploration and adoption of alternative fuels and technologies become increasingly critical. This chapter delves into the innovative solutions that are steering the industry away from fossil fuels and reducing its environmental footprint.

Electric vehicles (EVs) are at the forefront of this transformation. Tesla's rise to prominence with its all-electric lineup is a narrative of breaking barriers and altering consumer perceptions. The company's commitment to performance, range, and charging infrastructure has laid the groundwork for the widespread acceptance of EVs. Tesla's Model 3, for instance, has captured the market with its affordable pricing and robust features, making electric mobility accessible to a broader audience.

Beyond battery electric vehicles, plug-in hybrids (PHEVs) offer a bridge between traditional combustion engines and full electrification. Models like the Chevrolet Volt and the Toyota Prius Prime allow drivers to complete short journeys on electric power while retaining an internal combustion engine for longer trips. These vehicles provide a practical solution for consumers not ready to commit fully to electric vehicles, giving them a taste of what electric driving can offer.

Hydrogen fuel cell technology presents another avenue towards clean energy, with water vapor as the only emission. The Toyota Mirai and the Hyundai Nexo stand as examples of how hydrogen can power vehicles, offering quick refueling times and long-range capabilities. However, the scarcity of hydrogen refueling stations remains a challenge for widespread adoption.

In the pursuit of alternative fuels, biofuels continue to play a significant role. Made from renewable resources like plant biomass or animal fats, biofuels such as ethanol and biodiesel can reduce carbon emissions significantly. The Flex-Fuel vehicles, capable of running on high-ethanol blends, provide a practical alternative and are particularly popular in countries like Brazil, which has an extensive network of ethanol fuel stations.

Furthering the pursuit of sustainability, researchers and manufacturers are experimenting with synthetic fuels, also known as e-fuels. These are manufactured using carbon captured from the air, combined with hydrogen produced from renewable energy. Companies like Porsche are investing in the development of synthetic fuels as a way to maintain the performance of combustion engines while reducing their environmental impact.

Electric vehicles (EVs) are emerging as a cornerstone of alternative automotive technologies, challenging traditional transportation paradigms. Pioneers like Tesla have not only improved battery life and performance but have also made significant strides in the scalability of EV production. The Model S, with its high-performance battery pack, provides a range that competes with internal combustion engines, effectively addressing one of the most significant barriers to EV adoption: range anxiety. The adoption of EVs is further supported by global initiatives to expand charging infrastructure, exemplified by the growth of networks like ChargePoint and Tesla's Supercharger stations.

But the realm of EVs is not the only one witnessing revolutionary change. The plug-in hybrid vehicle (PHEV) market is flourishing, providing consumers with a transitional technology that combines the familiarity of gasoline engines with the benefits of electric propulsion. The Mitsubishi Outlander PHEV, for example, became Europe's best-selling PHEV, appealing to those who are not yet ready to abandon gasoline but are eager to reduce their carbon footprint.

Hydrogen fuel cells offer another promising direction, with vehicles like the Toyota Mirai showcasing the potential for a future where cars emit nothing but water. While the infrastructure for hydrogen fueling is in nascent stages, projects like California's Hydrogen Highway and Japan's Hydrogen Society Roadmap provide a glimpse into a concerted effort to establish hydrogen as a viable alternative fuel.

Biofuels also play a crucial role in the current energy transition. Ethanol, derived from crops like corn and sugarcane, has become a staple fuel in countries such as Brazil, where flex-fuel vehicles dominate the market. Biodiesel, another renewable option, is made from animal fats or vegetable oils and can be used in diesel engines with little to no modifications. Both fuels offer the advantage of utilizing existing internal combustion engine technologies while still providing reductions in carbon emissions.

The innovation in alternative fuels is paralleled by advances in automotive technologies. Start-stop systems, which turn off the engine at idle to save fuel, have become widespread. Continuously variable transmissions (CVTs) and advanced dual-clutch transmissions offer improved efficiency over traditional automatic transmissions.

The automotive industry's future is not without its hurdles. The development of sustainable and economically viable alternative fuels requires overcoming significant technological and logistical challenges. In addition, the industry must navigate complex regulatory environments and varying global standards for emissions and fuel economy.

Synthetic and e-fuels represent the next frontier, offering compatibility with existing internal combustion engines while significantly reducing emissions. Porsche's investment in the development of synthetic fuels, which could allow classic and current combustion engine cars to run without major modifications, is a testament to the potential of these fuels in preserving automotive heritage while aligning with modern environmental standards.

In parallel, the advancements in battery technology are crucial. Solid-state batteries are on the horizon, promising greater energy densities, faster charging times, and enhanced safety. Companies like Toyota and QuantumScape are at the forefront of this research, potentially revolutionizing the EV market.

The challenges facing alternative fuels and technologies are as diverse as the solutions. Infrastructure remains a critical issue, particularly for hydrogen and EVs. Battery disposal and recycling are other concerns that need addressing to prevent creating a new environmental problem while solving another.

Further discussions in the chapter would delve into the policies and incentives that different governments are employing to promote the use of alternative fuels and technologies. For instance, Norway's extensive tax incentives for EVs have resulted in one of the highest per capita rates of EV ownership in the world.

As we explore these developments, it becomes evident that the transition to alternative fuels is not solely a technological challenge but a comprehensive shift involving economic, social, and political change. The chapter would thus analyze the role of public perception and consumer behavior in the adoption of new automotive technologies. Surveys and studies that reflect public attitudes toward EVs, PHEVs, and hydrogen vehicles could provide insights into market trends and adoption rates.

Understanding the shift towards alternative fuels and technologies requires examining the cutting edge of automotive innovation and the broader energy ecosystem supporting it.

Electric vehicles (EVs) have rapidly moved from the margins to the mainstream, with companies like Tesla, Nissan, and Chevrolet leading the charge. Tesla's vehicles have been particularly transformative, combining long-range capabilities with high-performance features. The Tesla Model S set new standards for EVs with its impressive range and luxury status, while the more affordable Model 3 has brought electric cars to a wider audience.

Plug-in hybrid electric vehicles (PHEVs) like the Mitsubishi Outlander PHEV offer the comfort of a conventional gasoline engine with the option of electric driving. They provide a practical solution for consumers who desire improved fuel efficiency but are concerned about the purely electric range and charging infrastructure.

Hydrogen fuel cell vehicles represent another alternative, characterized by their fast refueling times and long range. The Toyota Mirai and the Hyundai Nexo showcase this technology with their sleek designs and zero-emission powertrains. However, the hydrogen fueling infrastructure remains limited, presenting a significant challenge to widespread adoption.

Biofuels have long been part of the alternative fuel conversation, with ethanol and biodiesel allowing for cleaner combustion. The success of flex-fuel vehicles, particularly in Brazil, illustrates the potential of biofuels to integrate into the current fueling infrastructure. Advances in second-generation biofuels, which are derived from non-food biomass, promise even greater reductions in life-cycle greenhouse gas emissions.

Synthetic fuels, or e-fuels, offer the possibility of carbon-neutral combustion and are particularly appealing for their ability to leverage existing fuel distribution systems. Companies like Porsche are investing in synthetic fuel production, exploring ways to create fuels that are both environmentally friendly and compatible with traditional engines.

These developments are set against a backdrop of continued innovation in vehicle technologies. Advancements in start-stop systems, transmission efficiency, and aerodynamic design are contributing to lower fuel consumption across vehicle classes. Lightweight materials, such as carbon fiber and advanced alloys, are reducing vehicle weight and enhancing fuel efficiency.

The challenge of integrating these diverse technologies into a cohesive and sustainable automotive strategy is substantial. It involves not only technological breakthroughs but also infrastructure development, market incentives, and regulatory frameworks. Policymakers and industry leaders must navigate these complex factors to advance the adoption of alternative fuels and technologies.

The chapter concludes by looking at the future of alternative fuels and automotive technologies. It examines emerging research in areas such as solid-state batteries, wireless charging, and next-generation biofuels. The narrative acknowledges the challenges ahead but remains optimistic about the role of innovation in driving the automotive industry towards a more sustainable future.

7

Policy and Regulatory Frameworks

Policy and regulatory frameworks play a pivotal role in shaping the sustainability of the automotive industry. Governments around the world have introduced a variety of regulations and incentives to encourage the production and adoption of environmentally friendly vehicles and to curb the negative environmental impacts of transportation.

In the European Union, the Euro 6 standards, implemented in 2014, have set strict limits on vehicle emissions, significantly reducing the allowable limits of nitrogen oxide (NOx) and particulate matter (PM) emitted by new vehicles. The EU's commitment to these standards has spurred automakers to innovate cleaner technologies, with companies like Volkswagen and Renault leading the way in developing engines that comply with these stringent regulations.

The United States has its own set of regulatory measures, such as the Corporate Average Fuel Economy (CAFE) standards, which aim to improve the average fuel economy of cars and light trucks sold in the U.S. In response, General Motors and Ford have invested in lightweight materials and efficient engine designs to meet these fuel efficiency goals.

In addition to these measures, the U.S. has also seen the implementation of the Zero Emission Vehicle (ZEV) program, initially adopted by California and later by other states, which requires manufacturers to sell a certain number of zero-emission vehicles. This has been a significant driving force behind the development and increased sales of EVs in the U.S., with Tesla's Model S, Chevrolet's Bolt EV, and Nissan's Leaf being among the most popular.

China, the world's largest car market, has implemented a dual-credit policy that requires carmakers to obtain a new energy vehicle (NEV) score, which can be earned by producing electric cars. China's aggressive policies have made it a global leader in the adoption of electric vehicles, with companies like BYD and NIO emerging as major players in the field.

Incentives play a crucial role in promoting the adoption of sustainable vehicles. Norway offers a prime example of how government policies can shape consumer behavior. The country provides extensive incentives for EV buyers, including exemptions from purchase taxes, road tolls, and parking fees. As a result, Norway has the highest per capita number of all-electric cars in the world.

The complexity of implementing effective automotive policy and regulatory frameworks lies not only in legislating but also in the careful balance of stakeholder interests and long-term environmental objectives. Japan's approach to fostering a hydrogen economy serves as a leading example of this balance. The government has outlined a comprehensive strategy that includes subsidies for fuel cell vehicles, investment in hydrogen refueling stations, and partnerships with local industries. The Toyota Mirai, as a beneficiary of this policy, symbolizes Japan's ambition to lead the world in hydrogen fuel cell technology.

The interplay between regulation and technology is also evident in policies aimed at reducing vehicle weight to improve fuel efficiency. The EU's end-of-life vehicle (ELV) directive, for example, requires that vehicles be designed for recyclability, and a certain percentage of the vehicle by weight must be recyclable. This directive has been influential in automakers' decisions to innovate with lightweight materials that also conform to these recyclability requirements.

Taxation is another tool governments use to influence automotive design and consumer choices. The UK, for instance, has adopted a graduated vehicle excise duty (VED) that varies according to CO2 emissions levels, encouraging consumers to purchase vehicles with lower emissions. This tax structure, along with grants for low-emission vehicles, has played a role in shaping consumer demand towards more sustainable vehicle options.

In the United States, the Renewable Fuel Standard (RFS) program requires a certain volume of renewable fuel to replace or reduce the quantity of petroleum-based transportation fuel, heating oil, or jet fuel. Programs like the RFS not only incentivize the production of biofuels but also encourage the automotive industry to develop vehicles compatible with these fuels.

Global initiatives also influence national policies. The Global Fuel Economy Initiative (GFEI), for example, aims to improve the fuel economy of the world's vehicles, with a particular focus on light-duty vehicles. It serves as a platform for sharing best practices and collaborating on strategies to reduce fuel consumption and greenhouse gas emissions from vehicles around the world.

In developing nations, where the growth of the automotive sector is accelerating, policy plays a crucial role in mitigating potential environmental impacts. India's Bharat Stage (BS) emission standards, for example, are government-mandated emission standards that were first introduced in 2000. With the implementation of BS-VI in 2020, which is comparable to Euro 6 standards, India has taken significant steps toward reducing vehicular pollution.

Additionally, the push for sustainability in the automotive sector is often accompanied by policies that encourage the development of domestic industries and reduce reliance on imports. In Brazil, the Inovar-Auto program was established to incentivize the production of more energy-efficient vehicles and stimulate the use of national automotive parts, combining economic and environmental objectives.

As national governments and international bodies grapple with the pressing issue of climate change, the automotive sector has come under increased scrutiny. Legislative measures across various countries have been instrumental in curbing vehicular emissions and promoting cleaner technologies.

In the European Union, the introduction of CO_2 emission performance standards for new cars has had a significant impact. These standards set out average emission targets for new vehicles, with heavy fines imposed on manufacturers that fail to comply. The success of these regulations can be partly attributed to the substantial decrease in average CO_2 emissions from new cars registered in the EU, despite the growing market share of SUVs, which typically have higher emissions.

Across the Atlantic, the California Air Resources Board (CARB) has been pivotal in pushing for cleaner cars through its Advanced Clean Cars Program. This program not only targets greenhouse gas emissions but also mandates an increase in the production and sale of zero-emission vehicles (ZEVs), creating a domino effect that influences other states and even federal policy.

China's approach to tackling the twin challenges of air pollution and greenhouse gas emissions from vehicles has been multifaceted. China's New Energy Vehicle (NEV) program is particularly noteworthy, offering subsidies for electric and hybrid vehicles, which has resulted in China becoming the largest market for these vehicles. The program's success is evident in the rapid growth of China's domestic EV market and the emergence of Chinese EV manufacturers as global competitors.

India's automotive sector is undergoing a transformation with the implementation of Bharat Stage VI (BS-VI) emission standards, which are among the strictest in the world. These standards have necessitated a leapfrogging in automotive technology, with many manufacturers revamping their product lines to comply.

In Brazil, the PROCONVE program, similar to the EU's emission standards, has been effective in reducing vehicular pollution. The program sets progressive emission limits for vehicles and has contributed to significant improvements in the country's air quality.

At the intersection of policy and technology, innovations such as Vehicle-to-Grid (V2G) systems are beginning to gain traction. V2G technology allows EVs to return energy to the power grid, potentially stabilizing the grid during peak demand or fluctuations in renewable energy generation. Policymakers are beginning to explore incentives for V2G-capable vehicles, recognizing the broader benefits of integrating transportation with smart grid technologies.

In terms of fuel economy, Japan has been at the forefront with its Top Runner Program. This innovative approach sets efficiency standards based on the best-performing models in each vehicle category, pushing manufacturers to continually innovate to remain competitive.

The fuel economy and emissions regulations have also driven advancements in internal combustion engine (ICE) technology. Manufacturers have developed engines that are both smaller and more powerful, often through the use of turbocharging and direct fuel injection. The resulting engines not only meet stringent environmental standards but also deliver the performance that consumers demand.

The discussion on policy and regulatory frameworks must also address the intricacies of emissions testing protocols, which have been under intense scrutiny in recent years. Following the revelation of emissions cheating by a major automaker, regulators worldwide have been compelled to tighten testing procedures to ensure that laboratory results reflect real-world driving conditions more accurately. The Worldwide Harmonized Light Vehicles Test Procedure (WLTP) is one such initiative, adopted by the European Union, which provides a more accurate basis for measuring a vehicle's fuel consumption and emissions.

While the WLTP represents a significant step forward, discrepancies between lab tests and on-road performance still exist. To bridge this gap, the Real Driving Emissions (RDE) test was introduced, requiring manufacturers to equip vehicles with Portable Emissions Measurement Systems (PEMS) to monitor pollutants like NOx during actual driving conditions on public roads.

The financial sector has also begun to play a role in shaping automotive sustainability. In response to the Paris Agreement, many banks and investors are reevaluating their investment strategies, with some opting to divest from companies that produce vehicles with high emissions. Green bonds and other financial instruments aimed at supporting sustainable practices in the automotive industry have gained popularity, reflecting a broader trend of integrating environmental considerations into financial decision-making.

Insurance companies are also adjusting policies to encourage the adoption of environmentally friendly vehicles. Lower premiums for EVs and hybrids, as well as discounts for vehicles with advanced safety features that can reduce the likelihood of accidents, are examples of market-based incentives aligned with sustainability goals.

Looking at the global landscape, the International Energy Agency (IEA) plays a crucial role in coordinating international energy policies, including those affecting the automotive sector. Its technology roadmaps and policy recommendations provide guidance for governments seeking to transition to cleaner automotive technologies. The IEA's global outlook reports offer comprehensive analysis and forecasting, influencing policymakers worldwide.

Finally, the role of non-governmental organizations (NGOs) and consumer advocacy groups cannot be overlooked. These entities are instrumental in raising public awareness about the environmental impacts of vehicles, lobbying for stricter regulations, and holding manufacturers accountable for their environmental claims. Groups like the International Council on Clean Transportation (ICCT) provide independent research and technical analysis that help shape policy decisions.

8

The Role of Consumers in Driving Change

Consumers play a pivotal role in driving change within the automotive industry. Their preferences, buying patterns, and social consciousness shape market trends and, in turn, influence how car manufacturers respond with product offerings.

In recent years, there has been a marked shift in consumer behavior towards environmentally friendly vehicles. The surge in demand for electric vehicles (EVs), for example, is a direct result of consumer awareness of climate change issues and a desire for sustainable lifestyles. In Norway, generous government incentives, coupled with high environmental awareness among consumers, have led to EVs accounting for a significant share of new car sales.

In the United States, the popularity of Tesla's Model 3 is another example of consumers making a clear choice for sustainability. Despite lacking the extensive history and dealer networks of established car manufacturers, Tesla has become a market leader, largely due to consumer advocacy and word-of-mouth marketing.

Car-sharing and ride-sharing services have gained popularity as consumers increasingly prioritize access over ownership. Services like Zipcar and peer-to-peer platforms like Turo have capitalized on this trend, which not only reflects changing attitudes towards car ownership but also helps reduce the number of vehicles on the road, leading to lower emissions.

The movement towards sustainability is also seen in the rise of ethical consumption. Consumers are increasingly interested in the provenance of the vehicles they purchase — the materials used, the conditions under which they were produced, and the environmental footprint of the manufacturing process. This shift has encouraged automakers to adopt more transparent and responsible supply chain practices. For instance, Volvo's commitment to traceability of cobalt used in its batteries is a response to consumer concerns about the ethical sourcing of raw materials.

Consumers are not only influencing the market through direct purchases but are also leveraging their collective voice through social media and other platforms to demand greater corporate responsibility. Campaigns and boycotts have the power to affect a company's brand and bottom line, compelling them to prioritize sustainable practices.

In some regions, consumer-driven demand for greener vehicles is also influenced by urban air quality concerns. In India, for instance, where cities are facing severe air pollution challenges, there is growing consumer interest in air quality and emission standards, which is beginning to be reflected in vehicle purchase patterns.

Looking at the global landscape, it is clear that consumer preferences can vary significantly by region. In many European cities, there is a strong push for cycling and public transportation as alternatives to personal car use. In contrast, in some areas of North America, where urban sprawl is more common, there is a greater demand for fuel-efficient SUVs and trucks.

Consumer advocacy has become an increasingly powerful force in shaping industry practices, with individuals and groups pushing for more transparency and higher environmental standards. Activism through platforms like social media has resulted in campaigns that can quickly gain traction and lead to tangible changes. The #BoycottDirtyDiesel campaign, for example, galvanized consumer sentiment against vehicles contributing to urban smog, influencing several cities to propose diesel bans.

The influence of consumers is also reflected in the growing market for sustainably produced vehicle components. The rise in popularity of synthetic leather interiors, made from recycled plastics or engineered fabrics, showcases consumer preference for cruelty-free and environmentally conscious options. Luxury automakers like BMW and Mercedes-Benz have introduced vegan interior options in response to consumer demand, marking a shift in how luxury is defined in the automotive industry.

Consumer data is shaping the future of the automotive landscape as well. Through the collection and analysis of vast amounts of data, companies are beginning to understand consumer preferences on a granular level. This data informs everything from vehicle design to service offerings. For instance, the preference for smartphone integration has led to the standardization of systems like Apple CarPlay and Android Auto across many models and brands.

The chapter would continue by examining the role of consumer-driven certifications and labels in promoting sustainability. Programs like the U.S. Environmental Protection Agency's (EPA) SmartWay, which identifies cleaner, more efficient vehicles, provide consumers with the information necessary to make informed choices. Similarly, the European Union energy label, providing clear energy consumption ratings, allows consumers to compare the environmental impact of their vehicle choices directly.

Moreover, the growing consumer demand for sustainable mobility has spurred the development of online platforms and apps that facilitate more informed decision-making. Websites like Carboncounter.com, developed by MIT researchers, allow consumers to compare cars based on their climate impact and lifetime costs, further empowering consumers to make choices that align with their environmental values.

As consumer preferences evolve, the automotive industry is observing a notable shift toward personalization and customization, reflecting individual values and environmental concerns. Electric vehicle manufacturers, in particular, are leveraging technology to offer a more personalized driving experience. For example, Tesla's over-the-air software updates allow drivers to customize their vehicle's performance and features, aligning with the owner's driving style and efficiency preferences.

This consumer influence extends to the used car market as well, where the resale value of cars is increasingly affected by their environmental performance. Vehicles with poor fuel economy or high emissions are seeing steeper depreciation rates, reflecting the market's growing preference for sustainability. This trend encourages manufacturers to consider the long-term environmental impact of their vehicles from the design stage, knowing that today's new car is tomorrow's used car.

In emerging markets, the rapid urbanization and the burgeoning middle class are creating new consumer segments. These consumers often exhibit heightened environmental consciousness, influenced by the visible effects of pollution in dense urban areas. In response, automakers are introducing models that are not only affordable but also environmentally friendly. For instance, India's Tata Motors has introduced the Nexon EV, an affordable electric SUV, which has been well-received by consumers looking for sustainable mobility options.

The rise of electric micro-mobility solutions, such as e-bikes and e-scooters, is also a consumer-driven phenomenon. Urban commuters, particularly in Europe and Asia, are embracing these alternatives for short-distance travel, prompting automotive companies to diversify their portfolios. Recognizing the potential of this trend, traditional car manufacturers like BMW and Audi have started to invest in electric micro-mobility solutions, broadening their roles from car manufacturers to comprehensive mobility service providers.

As the chapter progresses, it becomes evident that consumers are not just passive recipients in the automotive market; they are active participants with the power to influence the industry's direction. Their collective action, whether through purchasing decisions, social media advocacy, or participation in sharing economies, is reshaping the automotive landscape.

Yet, the effectiveness of consumer influence can sometimes be limited by economic factors. The initial higher cost of electric vehicles, despite lower operating costs, can be a barrier for many consumers. To address this, some governments have introduced incentive programs, such as rebates and tax credits, to reduce the economic burden on consumers and encourage the transition to clean energy vehicles. These policy measures not only support consumer choice but also signal government commitment to environmental sustainability, creating a positive feedback loop that further empowers consumer influence.

As more consumers demand sustainable practices and products, companies are compelled to innovate to meet these expectations. This innovation isn't limited to the vehicles themselves but also encompasses the entire customer experience, from sales and service to the aftermarket.

For instance, online car sales platforms are becoming increasingly popular, offering consumers a more transparent and low-pressure sales environment. These platforms often provide detailed information about the environmental performance of vehicles, allowing consumers to make decisions aligned with their sustainability values from the comfort of their own homes.

The future of the automotive industry, as influenced by consumer behavior, is likely to see a continued push towards more personalized, environmentally friendly, and interconnected mobility solutions. These trends suggest a vibrant and dynamic future for the sector, one in which consumer choice plays a central role in driving innovation and sustainability.

The role of consumers in driving change within the automotive industry cannot be understated. Their collective preferences and individual choices have a powerful impact, pushing the industry towards a more sustainable and environmentally conscious future. As the narrative of this chapter unfolds, it is clear that the role of consumers will remain a potent force in shaping the trajectory of the automotive industry.

The consumer's push for sustainable transportation extends beyond the vehicles themselves to the broader context in which they are used. Urban planning and the development of smart cities are influenced by consumer demand for integrated, efficient, and green transportation systems. Cities are being redesigned with a focus on reducing the reliance on personal vehicles, instead promoting public transit, cycling, and walking — all shaped by consumer advocacy for a cleaner environment.

This shift is palpable in the rise of e-mobility as a service (eMaaS) platforms. Services like Moovit and Citymapper integrate public transportation, ride-sharing, and bike-sharing into a single app, offering consumers a convenient way to choose the most efficient and sustainable route. These platforms illustrate how consumer demand for convenience and efficiency can align with environmental benefits.

The insurance industry, too, is responding to consumer-led changes. Usage-based insurance (UBI) models, where premiums are tied to vehicle usage patterns, promote less driving and incentivize consumers to opt for alternative transportation options. As a result, consumers are not only rewarded for driving less but also for adopting safer and more environmentally conscious driving behaviors.

Furthermore, the increasing consumer concern about the carbon footprint of vehicle production has led to a greater focus on the supply chain's sustainability. Consumers are demanding more information about the origin of the components in their vehicles, driving automakers to pursue greater transparency and sustainability in their supply chains. This has led to initiatives like the Responsible Sourcing Blockchain Network (RSBN), which aims to increase transparency in the mineral sourcing for batteries.

Within the industry, there is a recognition that future success hinges on aligning business strategies with consumer values. This is evident in the rise of Corporate Social Responsibility (CSR) reporting, with companies like Volvo and Ford publishing detailed reports on their sustainability efforts, not only to inform consumers but also to demonstrate their commitment to these values.

The current scenario shows how a new generation of consumers is looking beyond the product itself to the corporate ethos of car manufacturers. They favor companies that take tangible actions to address environmental challenges and that engage in community development and global sustainability efforts.

The role of consumers extends far into the realm of policy influence. Grassroots movements and consumer advocacy groups are increasingly effective in lobbying for changes in environmental policy related to transportation. Their impact is seen in the strengthening of emissions regulations, the expansion of low-emission zones in cities, and the increase in funding for sustainable transportation infrastructure.

In detailing the interplay between consumers and the automotive industry, it paints a picture of a dynamic relationship. Consumers are not merely choosing products based on personal preference but are actively engaging with and shaping the industry through their values and demands. This relationship drives the development of new technologies, the formation of policies, and the reshaping of markets.

Consumers are integral to the sustainable transformation of the automotive industry. Their decisions and demands have far-reaching implications, propelling the industry toward an increasingly sustainable future, underpinned by innovation, responsibility, and a commitment to environmental stewardship.

There is the influence of consumers on the aftermarket and repair industries, which are adapting to the sustainability trend. The growing popularity of upcycling and retrofitting older vehicles with new, cleaner technology—like converting classic cars to electric power—highlights a niche but growing segment of the market driven by eco-conscious consumers.

Attention to the life cycle of vehicles has also spurred an increase in recycling and remanufacturing programs, where parts are refurbished and reused, extending their life and reducing waste. Companies like Renault have invested in dedicated facilities for this purpose, signaling the industry's response to consumer concerns about waste.

Consumer impact on corporate governance and investment would be another focal point. Shareholder activism, where investors push for more sustainable practices from within, is prompting automakers to rethink their strategies. In some cases, it leads to divestment from activities that are not aligned with green objectives or to increased investment in sustainable technologies.

The consumer advocacy shapes the future of automotive industry jobs. The shift to green manufacturing and the demand for new technologies create opportunities for new careers and require a workforce skilled in sustainability practices.

By providing a multi-faceted look at how consumers influence every aspect of the automotive ecosystem—from design to decommissioning—the chapter offers a comprehensive analysis of their central role in driving sustainable change in the industry.

9

Future Trends and Innovations

The automotive industry stands on the cusp of a revolution, with emerging trends and innovations that promise to redefine mobility. Electrification, autonomy, and connectivity are not just buzzwords but are becoming tangible features of modern transportation. In this chapter, we examine the future of automotive design and technology, illustrating these concepts with real-world examples.

Electrification extends beyond passenger cars to commercial vehicles and public transportation. Companies like Tesla with their Semi, and newcomers like Rivian, which has received substantial investments for its electric delivery vans, are paving the way for a future where even heavy goods vehicles are electric. On the public transportation front, cities like

Shenzhen in China have completely electrified their bus fleets, signaling a commitment to clean urban transport.

Autonomous driving technology continues to advance, with industry leaders like Waymo and newcomers such as Zoox unveiling increasingly sophisticated systems. These technologies have the potential not only to improve safety but also to revolutionize car ownership, giving rise to shared mobility concepts that could reduce the number of vehicles on the roads.

Connectivity is another trend transforming the industry, as vehicles become part of the Internet of Things (IoT). Manufacturers like BMW and General Motors are integrating vehicles with smart home devices, allowing for seamless control and communication. This connectivity also facilitates the collection of data, which can be used to optimize traffic flows, reduce congestion, and enhance vehicle maintenance.

Sustainability remains a core focus, with innovations in materials and manufacturing processes. Research into bio-based composites, for instance, is leading to lighter and more environmentally friendly vehicle components. BMW's use of carbon fiber reinforced plastic in its i3 and i8 models is an example of how manufacturers are incorporating sustainable materials without compromising on performance or safety.

Another burgeoning field is the development of synthetic fuels and advanced biofuels, which aim to provide renewable alternatives to traditional fossil fuels. Companies like Audi are investing in e-fuels, which can be synthesized from CO_2 and hydrogen produced using renewable energy.

In urban planning, the concept of "mobility as a service" (MaaS) is taking hold. This approach views transportation as a comprehensive service that should be tailored to the needs of individuals and communities. Helsinki's Whim app, which allows users to access and pay for a range of transportation options, from buses and trains to bikes and taxis, embodies this trend.

As we forge ahead, vehicle-to-vehicle (V2V) and vehicle-to-infrastructure (V2I) communications emerge as key components in the next wave of automotive advancements. These technologies, collectively known as V2X, allow vehicles to communicate with each other and with road infrastructure, enhancing safety and traffic management. For example, in the event of an accident or traffic congestion, V2X technology can alert approaching vehicles to adjust their routes or speeds accordingly. Trials in cities like Pittsburgh and Singapore are actively testing these systems, with the latter aiming to leverage V2X to support its Smart Nation initiative.

The personalization of vehicles is also a trend gaining momentum. Future vehicles will likely offer greater customization options, adapting to user preferences and needs. Using artificial intelligence, cars will adjust seating, climate control, and entertainment options based on the driver's profile, a concept that is being explored by Mercedes-Benz with its MBUX infotainment system.

In terms of propulsion, while electric power is at the forefront, there is ongoing research into alternative energy sources. Hydrogen fuel cells, which have long promised a clean alternative to internal combustion engines, are seeing renewed interest with advancements in fuel cell technology and infrastructure. Toyota continues to invest in its Mirai, betting on hydrogen as a complementary technology to battery-electric vehicles, particularly in markets like Japan and California.

The integration of renewable energy into vehicle design is another innovative trend. Companies like Lightyear and Sono Motors are developing solar-powered cars, with integrated photovoltaic cells that can either supplement the vehicle's power needs or, in some cases, provide all the necessary energy for short trips.

On the manufacturing side, advancements in 3D printing are enabling more efficient production of complex parts, potentially revolutionizing supply chains and reducing waste. Local Motors, for example, has utilized 3D printing to produce its Strati vehicle, demonstrating the feasibility of this technology in automotive manufacturing.

Moreover, the push for circular economy principles is leading to new approaches in vehicle design and material use. The concept of designing for disassembly, where vehicles are created with the end-of-life recycling in mind, is being adopted by manufacturers like Volvo, which aims to have at least 25% of the plastics used in its cars be made from recycled materials by 2025.

The chapter continues by examining how these trends are not only driven by technological innovation but also by shifts in societal attitudes towards mobility, sustainability, and the shared economy. The rise of car-sharing platforms, the popularity of cycling in urban centers, and the increasing demand for public transit solutions are just a few examples of how consumer behavior is influencing the direction of the automotive industry.

As autonomous technology advances, ethical considerations come into focus. The industry is grappling with questions around decision-making algorithms in autonomous vehicles and their implications for safety and liability. This ongoing dialogue includes stakeholders from various sectors, including technology, automotive, legal, and ethical scholars.

The fusion of automotive technology with advanced materials science is opening up new horizons for vehicle efficiency and performance. The exploration of graphene-based materials, known for their extraordinary strength and conductivity, could lead to the next generation of batteries with faster charging times and longer life spans. Research into these materials is being spearheaded by institutions and companies worldwide, with the potential to greatly enhance the electric vehicle's appeal and performance.

Adaptive and active materials are also gaining interest, which could lead to vehicles with surfaces that respond dynamically to environmental conditions. For example, materials that change texture to reduce drag at high speeds or that can self-heal minor scratches and dents are under development. These materials would not only contribute to the aesthetic and functional aspects of the vehicle but also enhance its sustainability by extending its lifespan and reducing maintenance needs.

Digitalization of the automotive industry is another irreversible trend. Digital twin technology, which creates a virtual model of a physical vehicle, allows engineers to simulate and optimize designs and operations before a single physical prototype is built. This technology reduces the time and resources required for development and can be seen in action in Formula 1, where race teams use digital twins to optimize the performance of their cars from race to race.

The automotive industry's future will likely be shaped significantly by advancements in artificial intelligence (AI). AI is expected to enhance various aspects of the automotive experience, from autonomous driving and predictive maintenance to personalized in-car services. AI algorithms are improving at interpreting the vast amounts of data generated by vehicles, making driving safer and more efficient. Automakers like Ford and Volkswagen are investing heavily in AI to lead the development of intelligent vehicles.

In terms of innovation in automotive services, there is a significant push towards creating an ecosystem that extends beyond the vehicle itself. For example, Tesla's Supercharger network is not just about providing charging stations but also about creating a seamless and integrated service experience for the user, potentially incorporating solar power generation and battery storage.

Sustainability in transportation is increasingly being viewed through the lens of urban and societal health. The proliferation of low-emission zones in cities is pushing for cleaner transportation options. Bicycles and e-scooters are being integrated into urban mobility strategies, reducing reliance on cars for short-distance travel. In response to these trends, automotive companies are diversifying their offerings, as seen with GM's investment in e-bike startup Ariv and Uber's acquisition of e-bike and e-scooter company Jump.

Looking at the broader environmental impact, there is a growing emphasis on the decarbonization of the entire life cycle of vehicles. This approach includes not just the tailpipe emissions but also the carbon footprint of manufacturing, operation, and end-of-life disposal. Lifecycle assessment tools are becoming more sophisticated, allowing manufacturers and consumers alike to understand the full environmental impact of their vehicles.

These future trends and innovations suggest a shift in the automotive industry towards integrated, intelligent, and sustainable solutions. As the chapter unfolds, it becomes clear that the industry is not just responding to technological opportunities but is also proactively seeking to redefine the very concept of mobility in alignment with broader environmental and social goals.

10

Building a Sustainable Automotive Industry

Building a sustainable automotive industry is a multifaceted challenge that extends beyond reducing tailpipe emissions to encompass the entire lifecycle of a vehicle, from design and manufacturing to operation and end-of-life recycling.

The path to sustainability starts with vehicle design. Automakers are increasingly employing life cycle assessment (LCA) tools to understand the environmental impact of their vehicles from cradle to grave. The use of sustainable materials such as recycled plastics, biocomposites, and lighter metals contributes to reducing the overall carbon footprint. For instance, the BMW i3, constructed with a carbon-fiber-reinforced polymer, has set a benchmark for sustainable car design.

Manufacturing processes are also under transformation. Car manufacturers are adopting green manufacturing techniques, which include the utilization of renewable energy sources, such as solar and wind, in their production plants. Companies like Volkswagen and General Motors have made significant commitments to powering their manufacturing operations with 100% renewable energy within the next decade.

Another pillar of building a sustainable industry is the development and promotion of cleaner fuels and advanced powertrain technologies. The electrification of the vehicle fleet is underway, with companies like Tesla, Nissan, and BYD leading the charge. Simultaneously, the development of hydrogen fuel cell technology, supported by companies like Toyota with their Mirai model, offers another pathway towards a zero-emissions future.

To ensure the widespread adoption of electric vehicles, substantial investment in charging infrastructure is essential. Collaborative efforts such as the Ionity network in Europe, a joint venture between BMW, Ford, Mercedes, and Volkswagen, aim to build a comprehensive network of high-speed chargers across the continent.

In addition to infrastructure, fostering innovation in battery technology is crucial. Research into solid-state batteries and other advanced energy storage solutions holds the promise of safer, more efficient, and longer-lasting energy storage options. Companies like Solid Power and QuantumScape are at the forefront of this research, working towards commercializing these next-generation batteries.

The automotive industry is also looking at ways to extend the life of vehicles through remanufacturing and refurbishing programs. By designing vehicles that are easier to disassemble and recycle, manufacturers can reduce waste and preserve the value of materials. Volvo's ambition to have no single-use plastics in their operations and vehicles by 2025 is an example of this circular economy approach.

Consumer behavior plays a significant role in driving industry sustainability. As buyers increasingly prioritize environmental considerations in their vehicle purchases, automakers are responding with products that align with these values. The rise of mobility services, like car-sharing and ride-hailing, also reflect changing attitudes towards vehicle ownership and represent an opportunity to reduce the number of cars on the road.

Policy and regulation will continue to underpin efforts to build a sustainable automotive industry. Governments around the world are setting ambitious targets for reducing vehicle emissions and encouraging the transition to low-emission vehicles through a combination of mandates, incentives, and penalties.

Building a sustainable automotive industry is a shared responsibility, requiring collaboration among automakers, suppliers, governments, and consumers. Through innovation, investment, and a shared commitment to environmental stewardship, the industry can contribute to the global effort to mitigate climate change and move towards a more sustainable future.

Sustainability in the automotive industry also hinges on the development of smarter, more efficient logistics and supply chains. By optimizing routes, improving load management, and reducing unnecessary transportation, carbon emissions associated with the movement of parts and vehicles can be significantly decreased. Utilizing predictive analytics and real-time data, logistics can be transformed to be more responsive and less wasteful. For example, Toyota's Just-In-Time production system minimizes inventory levels and the associated storage, thereby reducing the resources required to produce vehicles.

In tandem with logistical improvements, there's a push towards localizing production to minimize transportation emissions. Automakers are opening plants closer to key markets. For instance, Tesla's Gigafactory in Shanghai brings production closer to the Asian market, reducing the carbon footprint associated with shipping vehicles overseas.

Technological advances also play a crucial role in enhancing driving efficiency and reducing the environmental impact during the vehicle's use phase. The integration of AI and machine learning in vehicles can optimize fuel consumption, route planning, and even driving patterns for better fuel efficiency. Advanced driver-assistance systems (ADAS) that improve vehicle safety also contribute to this efficiency by preventing accidents and the associated economic and environmental costs.

A key aspect of sustainability involves extending the lifespan of vehicles. Remanufacturing and refurbishing programs, as mentioned, can revitalize aging vehicles, but maintenance plays a critical part too. Manufacturers are exploring new service models that emphasize vehicle longevity. For instance, companies like Rivian offer a comprehensive maintenance package that includes remote diagnostics, reducing the need for physical service centers and the associated environmental footprint.

As electric vehicles become more prevalent, the end-of-life phase for batteries presents both a challenge and an opportunity. The automotive industry is exploring battery second-life applications, where used EV batteries are repurposed for stationary energy storage systems. Nissan and General Motors have initiated projects that demonstrate the viability of this approach, turning a potential environmental problem into a sustainable solution.

Collaboration extends to the end of the vehicle's life, where manufacturers are working with recycling companies to ensure that vehicles are disposed of in an environmentally responsible manner. Recycling not only reduces the need for virgin materials but also decreases landfill waste. Companies like Renault operate their own recycling programs, ensuring that materials from their vehicles are recovered and reused.

Sustainability is not just about environmental concerns but also about economic and social issues. The automotive industry is increasingly aware of its role in promoting social equity, providing fair wages, and ensuring that the benefits of green technologies are available to all segments of society. Through corporate social responsibility (CSR) initiatives and partnerships with governments and NGOs, the industry can support the development of a more equitable society.

Building a sustainable automotive industry is an endeavor that requires continuous innovation, collaboration, and a willingness to adapt to new challenges and opportunities. It is a comprehensive approach that touches on every aspect of the vehicle lifecycle and requires the collective effort of all stakeholders. As the industry evolves, it becomes clear that sustainability is not just a trend but an imperative for the long-term viability and success of the automotive sector.

The journey towards a sustainable automotive industry isn't just limited to the manufacturing of vehicles; it extends into the realm of after-sales services and customer experiences. Automakers are integrating green practices into their dealerships and service centers. For instance,

Ford's 'Go Green' dealership sustainability program aims to reduce the carbon footprint and energy costs of their dealers through eco-friendly building upgrades and practices.

Sustainability is also about inclusivity and ensuring that advancements in vehicle technology are accessible to all sectors of the population. Programs aimed at expanding EV ownership to low-income communities are examples of this, such as California's Clean Vehicle Rebate Project, which offers increased incentives for qualifying low-income applicants. Such initiatives are crucial in democratizing the benefits of green technologies.

In the global push for sustainability, cross-industry partnerships are proving vital. Automakers are collaborating with tech firms, energy companies, and even competitors to drive forward their sustainability agendas. These partnerships are crucial for sharing knowledge, resources, and innovation. For example, the collaboration between BMW and Toyota on hydrogen fuel cell technology shows how pooling expertise can accelerate development in areas crucial for sustainability.

At the same time, the development of sustainable urban environments is symbiotic with the evolution of the automotive industry. Smart city projects, which integrate transportation, housing, and energy systems, are becoming testbeds for new automotive technologies. The integration of autonomous electric shuttles in smart city environments, as seen with projects in cities like Columbus, Ohio, offers a view of how the urban landscape can adapt to and foster sustainable transportation solutions.

Moreover, education and consumer awareness campaigns play a significant role in building a sustainable industry. By informing potential buyers about the benefits and practicalities of sustainable vehicles, the industry can stimulate market demand and encourage the adoption of green technologies. Educational initiatives such as electric vehicle experience centers, where consumers can learn about and test drive EVs, are valuable tools in this effort.

In discussing the future, the potential of next-generation biofuels cannot be ignored. Research into cellulosic ethanol, derived from non-food plant materials, offers the possibility of biofuels that do not compete with food crops for arable land. This research is critical in ensuring the sustainability of biofuels and their role in the future energy mix for transportation.

Innovation in the automotive industry is also taking cues from other sectors. For instance, the principles of the circular economy, where waste is minimized, and materials are kept in use for as long as possible, are finding their way into vehicle design and manufacturing. The Renault-Nissan-Mitsubishi alliance is exploring circular economy concepts, from modular vehicle design that facilitates repairs to developing new business models around vehicle leasing and refurbishing.

Building a sustainable automotive industry is about more than just adopting green practices; it's about transforming the entire ethos of the industry. It's a commitment to continuous improvement, to listening to the needs of the planet, its people, and future generations. As this chapter draws to a close, it is clear that the pathway to sustainability is not straightforward, nor is it the effort of a single entity. It is a collaborative, innovative, and ongoing process that encompasses every aspect of the automotive industry.

As we reach the conclusion of our exploration into creating a sustainable automotive industry, it's clear that the journey is as complex as it is critical. The challenges are multifaceted, involving technological innovation, consumer behavior, policy reform, and a deep-seated commitment to environmental stewardship.

From the production lines that are reimagining the use of materials and energy, to the boardrooms where strategic decisions are made for the long-term health of the planet, sustainability is becoming an integral part of the automotive narrative. It's a story of transformation, of industries and consumers alike working towards a future that is not only viable but vibrant in its respect for the environment.

The electric hum of an EV, the collective efforts to reduce, reuse, and recycle, the policies shaping a cleaner future, and the consumers demanding responsibility — all are threads in the tapestry of change. Each innovation, from hydrogen fuel cells to AI-driven autonomous vehicles, each act of legislation, each conscious consumer choice, and each collaboration across sectors, contributes to the momentum towards a sustainable automotive era.

This book has endeavored to capture the spirit of this transition, examining the many facets of the industry's evolution. We've seen how the forces of change are as diverse as the global market itself, with each region contributing its unique challenges and solutions to the collective goal.

Looking ahead, the path to sustainability is one of perpetual progress. The industry must continue to innovate, adapt, and respond to the ever-changing environmental and social landscape. It will require vigilance, courage, and an unwavering commitment to the principles of sustainability — principles that must be woven into the very fabric of automotive culture and practice.

Building a sustainable automotive industry is more than a technical challenge; it's a global imperative, a social responsibility, and an economic opportunity. It calls for a shared vision for the future, one where technology, humanity, and the environment progress in harmony.

In conclusion, "Driving Change: Innovating Sustainability in the Automotive Industry" has embarked on a comprehensive journey through the many facets of sustainability in the automotive sector. From the emergence of alternative fuels and technologies to the integral role of policy and consumer advocacy, we have explored the numerous challenges and opportunities that lie ahead for an industry at a pivotal crossroads.

We began by laying the foundation with the history of the automotive industry, understanding the environmental impacts that have led to the current demand for sustainable practices. We then moved through the various innovative responses by industry leaders, witnessing the emergence of electric vehicles, advances in material science, and the inception of smarter, cleaner manufacturing processes.

The narrative of this book has underscored the importance of collaborative efforts across governments, industries, and consumers in driving the shift towards sustainability. It is clear that no single stakeholder can effect change in isolation. Instead, it is the concerted efforts of all parties, fueled by innovation and guided by stringent policy frameworks, that will steer the industry towards a greener future.

The examples from around the world have shown that while challenges persist, the resolve to overcome them is strong and widespread. Companies are reimagining their role, not just as carmakers but as providers of mobility solutions. Governments are crafting policies not just to regulate but also to inspire and facilitate change. And consumers are not just buyers but active participants in the movement towards a sustainable future.

As we look ahead, it is evident that the automotive industry's journey towards sustainability is an ongoing process, marked by continuous learning and adaptation. The roads ahead will be shaped by further technological breakthroughs, evolving policy landscapes, and the ever-changing tapestry of consumer preferences.

"Driving Change" concludes with a call to action for continued innovation, investment, and global cooperation. The industry's future will depend on its ability to embrace change, to remain resilient in the face of obstacles, and to keep sustainability at the core of its mission. The wheels of progress are in motion, and with each advancement, we move closer to a future where the automotive industry can proudly claim not just to have reduced its environmental footprint but to have enriched the global community and safeguarded the planet for generations to come.

www.ingramcontent.com/pod-product-compliance
Lightning Source LLC
Chambersburg PA
CBHW070818170726
48000CB00018B/1085